THE MOST IMPORTANT THING A MAN CAN GIVE TO GOD APART FROM HIS HEART.

THE MOST IMPORTANT THING A MAN CAN GIVE TO GOD APART FROM HIS HEART.

THE MOST IMPORTANT THING A MAN CAN GIVE TO GOD APART FROM HIS HEART

THE MOST IMPORTANT THING A MAN CAN GIVE TO
GOD APART FROM HIS HEART.

THE MOST IMPORTANT THING A MAN CAN GIVE TO GOD APART FROM HIS HEART

THE MOST IMPORTANT THING A MAN CAN GIVE TO GOD APART FROM HIS HEART.

THE MOST IMPORTANT THING A MAN CAN GIVE TO GOD APART FROM HIS HEART

THE MOST IMPORTANT THING A MAN CAN GIVE TO GOD APART FROM HIS HEART.

THE MOST IMPORTANT THING A MAN CAN GIVE TO GOD APART FROM HIS HEART

THE MOST IMPORTANT THING A MAN CAN GIVE TO GOD APART FROM HIS HEART.

THE MOST IMPORTANT THING A MAN CAN GIVE TO GOD APART FROM HIS HEART

THE MOST IMPORTANT THING A MAN CAN GIVE TO GOD APART FROM HIS HEART.

THE MOST IMPORTANT THING A MAN CAN GIVE TO GOD APART FROM HIS HEART

THE MOST IMPORTANT THING A MAN CAN GIVE TO GOD APART FROM HIS HEART.

THE MOST IMPORTANT THING A MAN CAN GIVE TO GOD APART FROM HIS HEART

THE MOST IMPORTANT THING A MAN CAN GIVE TO GOD APART FROM HIS HEART.

THE MOST IMPORTANT THING A MAN CAN GIVE TO GOD APART FROM HIS HEART

THE MOST IMPORTANT THING A MAN CAN GIVE TO GOD APART FROM HIS HEART.

THE MOST IMPORTANT THING A MAN CAN GIVE TO GOD APART FROM HIS HEART

THE MOST IMPORTANT THING A MAN CAN GIVE TO GOD APART FROM HIS HEART.

THE MOST IMPORTANT THING A MAN CAN GIVE TO GOD APART FROM HIS HEART

THE MOST IMPORTANT THING A MAN CAN GIVE TO GOD APART FROM HIS HEART.

THE MOST IMPORTANT THING A MAN CAN GIVE TO GOD APART FROM HIS HEART

THE MOST IMPORTANT THING A MAN CAN GIVE TO GOD APART FROM HIS HEART.

THE MOST IMPORTANT THING A MAN CAN GIVE TO GOD APART FROM HIS HEART

THE MOST IMPORTANT THING A MAN CAN GIVE TO GOD APART FROM HIS HEART.

THE MOST IMPORTANT THING A MAN CAN GIVE TO GOD APART FROM HIS HEART

THE MOST IMPORTANT THING A MAN CAN GIVE TO GOD APART FROM HIS HEART.

THE MOST IMPORTANT THING A MAN CAN GIVE TO GOD APART FROM HIS HEART

THE MOST IMPORTANT THING A MAN CAN GIVE TO GOD APART FROM HIS HEART.

THE MOST IMPORTANT THING A MAN CAN GIVE TO GOD APART FROM HIS HEART

THE MOST IMPORTANT THING A MAN CAN GIVE TO GOD APART FROM HIS HEART.

THE MOST IMPORTANT THING A MAN CAN GIVE TO GOD APART FROM HIS HEART

THE MOST IMPORTANT THING A MAN CAN GIVE TO GOD APART FROM HIS HEART.

THE MOST IMPORTANT THING A MAN CAN GIVE TO GOD APART FROM HIS HEART

THE MOST IMPORTANT THING A MAN CAN GIVE TO GOD APART FROM HIS HEART.

THE MOST IMPORTANT THING A MAN CAN GIVE TO GOD APART FROM HIS HEART

THE MOST IMPORTANT THING A MAN CAN GIVE TO GOD APART FROM HIS HEART.

THE MOST IMPORTANT THING A MAN CAN GIVE TO GOD APART FROM HIS HEART

THE MOST IMPORTANT THING A MAN CAN GIVE TO GOD APART FROM HIS HEART.

THE MOST IMPORTANT THING A MAN CAN GIVE TO GOD APART FROM HIS HEART

THE MOST IMPORTANT THING A MAN CAN GIVE TO GOD APART FROM HIS HEART.

THE MOST IMPORTANT THING A MAN CAN GIVE TO GOD APART FROM HIS HEART

THE MOST IMPORTANT THING A MAN CAN GIVE TO GOD APART FROM HIS HEART.

THE MOST IMPORTANT THING A MAN CAN GIVE TO GOD APART FROM HIS HEART

THE MOST IMPORTANT THING A MAN CAN GIVE TO GOD APART FROM HIS HEART.

THE MOST IMPORTANT THING A MAN CAN GIVE TO GOD APART FROM HIS HEART

THE MOST IMPORTANT THING A MAN CAN GIVE TO
GOD APART FROM HIS HEART.

THE MOST IMPORTANT THING A MAN CAN GIVE TO GOD APART FROM HIS HEART

THE MOST IMPORTANT THING A MAN CAN GIVE TO
GOD APART FROM HIS HEART.

THE MOST IMPORTANT THING A MAN CAN GIVE TO GOD APART FROM HIS HEART

THE MOST IMPORTANT THING A MAN CAN GIVE TO GOD APART FROM HIS HEART.

THE MOST IMPORTANT THING A MAN CAN GIVE TO GOD APART FROM HIS HEART

THE MOST IMPORTANT THING A MAN CAN GIVE TO GOD APART FROM HIS HEART.

THE MOST IMPORTANT THING A MAN CAN GIVE TO GOD APART FROM HIS HEART

THE MOST IMPORTANT THING A MAN CAN GIVE TO GOD APART FROM HIS HEART.

THE MOST IMPORTANT THING A MAN CAN GIVE TO GOD APART FROM HIS HEART

THE MOST IMPORTANT THING A MAN CAN GIVE TO GOD APART FROM HIS HEART.

THE MOST IMPORTANT THING A MAN CAN GIVE TO GOD APART FROM HIS HEART

THE MOST IMPORTANT THING A MAN CAN GIVE TO GOD APART FROM HIS HEART.

THE MOST IMPORTANT THING A MAN CAN GIVE TO GOD APART FROM HIS HEART

THE MOST IMPORTANT THING A MAN CAN GIVE TO GOD APART FROM HIS HEART.

THE MOST IMPORTANT THING A MAN CAN GIVE TO GOD APART FROM HIS HEART

THE MOST IMPORTANT THING A MAN CAN GIVE TO GOD APART FROM HIS HEART.

THE MOST IMPORTANT THING A MAN CAN GIVE TO GOD APART FROM HIS HEART

THE MOST IMPORTANT THING A MAN CAN GIVE TO GOD APART FROM HIS HEART.

THE MOST IMPORTANT THING A MAN CAN GIVE TO GOD APART FROM HIS HEART

THE MOST IMPORTANT THING A MAN CAN GIVE TO GOD APART FROM HIS HEART.

THE MOST IMPORTANT THING A MAN CAN GIVE TO GOD APART FROM HIS HEART

THE MOST IMPORTANT THING A MAN CAN GIVE TO GOD APART FROM HIS HEART.

THE MOST IMPORTANT THING A MAN CAN GIVE TO GOD APART FROM HIS HEART

THE MOST IMPORTANT THING A MAN CAN GIVE TO GOD APART FROM HIS HEART

THE MOST IMPORTANT THING A MAN CAN GIVE TO GOD APART FROM HIS HEART.

THE MOST IMPORTANT THING A MAN CAN GIVE TO GOD APART FROM HIS HEART

THE MOST IMPORTANT THING A MAN CAN GIVE TO GOD APART FROM HIS HEART.

THE MOST IMPORTANT THING A MAN CAN GIVE TO GOD APART FROM HIS HEART

THE MOST IMPORTANT THING A MAN CAN GIVE TO GOD APART FROM HIS HEART.

THE MOST IMPORTANT THING A MAN CAN GIVE TO GOD APART FROM HIS HEART

THE MOST IMPORTANT THING A MAN CAN GIVE TO GOD APART FROM HIS HEART.

THE MOST IMPORTANT THING A MAN CAN GIVE TO GOD APART FROM HIS HEART

THE MOST IMPORTANT THING A MAN CAN GIVE TO GOD APART FROM HIS HEART.

THE MOST IMPORTANT THING A MAN CAN GIVE TO GOD APART FROM HIS HEART

THE MOST IMPORTANT THING A MAN CAN GIVE TO GOD APART FROM HIS HEART.

THE MOST IMPORTANT THING A MAN CAN GIVE TO GOD APART FROM HIS HEART

THE MOST IMPORTANT THING A MAN CAN GIVE TO GOD APART FROM HIS HEART.

THE MOST IMPORTANT THING A MAN CAN GIVE TO GOD APART FROM HIS HEART

THE MOST IMPORTANT THING A MAN CAN GIVE TO GOD APART FROM HIS HEART.

THE MOST IMPORTANT THING A MAN CAN GIVE TO GOD APART FROM HIS HEART

THE MOST IMPORTANT THING A MAN CAN GIVE TO GOD APART FROM HIS HEART.

THE MOST IMPORTANT THING A MAN CAN GIVE TO GOD APART FROM HIS HEART

THE MOST IMPORTANT THING A MAN CAN GIVE TO GOD APART FROM HIS HEART.

THE MOST IMPORTANT THING A MAN CAN GIVE TO GOD APART FROM HIS HEART

THE MOST IMPORTANT THING A MAN CAN GIVE TO GOD APART FROM HIS HEART.

THE MOST IMPORTANT THING A MAN CAN GIVE TO GOD APART FROM HIS HEART

THE MOST IMPORTANT THING A MAN CAN GIVE TO GOD APART FROM HIS HEART.

THE MOST IMPORTANT THING A MAN CAN GIVE TO GOD APART FROM HIS HEART

THE MOST IMPORTANT THING A MAN CAN GIVE TO GOD APART FROM HIS HEART.

THE MOST IMPORTANT THING A MAN CAN GIVE TO GOD APART FROM HIS HEART

THE MOST IMPORTANT THING A MAN CAN GIVE TO GOD APART FROM HIS HEART.

THE MOST IMPORTANT THING A MAN CAN GIVE TO GOD APART FROM HIS HEART

THE MOST IMPORTANT THING A MAN CAN GIVE TO GOD APART FROM HIS HEART.

THE MOST IMPORTANT THING A MAN CAN GIVE TO GOD APART FROM HIS HEART

THE MOST IMPORTANT THING A MAN CAN GIVE TO GOD APART FROM HIS HEART.

THE MOST IMPORTANT THING A MAN CAN GIVE TO GOD APART FROM HIS HEART

THE MOST IMPORTANT THING A MAN CAN GIVE TO GOD APART FROM HIS HEART.

THE MOST IMPORTANT THING A MAN CAN GIVE TO GOD APART FROM HIS HEART

THE MOST IMPORTANT THING A MAN CAN GIVE TO GOD APART FROM HIS HEART.

THE MOST IMPORTANT THING A MAN CAN GIVE TO GOD APART FROM HIS HEART

THE MOST IMPORTANT THING A MAN CAN GIVE TO GOD APART FROM HIS HEART.

THE MOST IMPORTANT THING A MAN CAN GIVE TO GOD APART FROM HIS HEART

THE MOST IMPORTANT THING A MAN CAN GIVE TO GOD APART FROM HIS HEART.

THE MOST IMPORTANT THING A MAN CAN GIVE TO GOD APART FROM HIS HEART.

THE MOST IMPORTANT THING A MAN CAN GIVE TO GOD APART FROM HIS HEART

THE MOST IMPORTANT THING A MAN CAN GIVE TO GOD APART FROM HIS HEART.

THE MOST IMPORTANT THING A MAN CAN GIVE TO GOD APART FROM HIS HEART

THE MOST IMPORTANT THING A MAN CAN GIVE TO GOD APART FROM HIS HEART.

THE MOST IMPORTANT THING A MAN CAN GIVE TO GOD APART FROM HIS HEART

THE MOST IMPORTANT THING A MAN CAN GIVE TO GOD APART FROM HIS HEART.

THE MOST IMPORTANT THING A MAN CAN GIVE TO GOD APART FROM HIS HEART

THE MOST IMPORTANT THING A MAN CAN GIVE TO GOD APART FROM HIS HEART.

THE MOST IMPORTANT THING A MAN CAN GIVE TO GOD APART FROM HIS HEART

THE MOST IMPORTANT THING A MAN CAN GIVE TO GOD APART FROM HIS HEART.

THE MOST IMPORTANT THING A MAN CAN GIVE TO GOD APART FROM HIS HEART

THE MOST IMPORTANT THING A MAN CAN GIVE TO GOD APART FROM HIS HEART.

THE MOST IMPORTANT THING A MAN CAN GIVE TO GOD APART FROM HIS HEART

THE MOST IMPORTANT THING A MAN CAN GIVE TO GOD APART FROM HIS HEART.

THE MOST IMPORTANT THING A MAN CAN GIVE TO GOD APART FROM HIS HEART

THE MOST IMPORTANT THING A MAN CAN GIVE TO GOD APART FROM HIS HEART.

THE MOST IMPORTANT THING A MAN CAN GIVE TO GOD APART FROM HIS HEART.

THE MOST IMPORTANT THING A MAN CAN GIVE TO GOD APART FROM HIS HEART

THE MOST IMPORTANT THING A MAN CAN GIVE TO GOD APART FROM HIS HEART.

THE MOST IMPORTANT THING A MAN CAN GIVE TO GOD APART FROM HIS HEART

THE MOST IMPORTANT THING A MAN CAN GIVE TO GOD APART FROM HIS HEART.

THE MOST IMPORTANT THING A MAN CAN GIVE TO GOD APART FROM HIS HEART

THE MOST IMPORTANT THING A MAN CAN GIVE TO GOD APART FROM HIS HEART.

THE MOST IMPORTANT THING A MAN CAN GIVE TO GOD APART FROM HIS HEART

THE MOST IMPORTANT THING A MAN CAN GIVE TO GOD APART FROM HIS HEART.

THE MOST IMPORTANT THING A MAN CAN GIVE TO GOD APART FROM HIS HEART

THE MOST IMPORTANT THING A MAN CAN GIVE TO GOD APART FROM HIS HEART.

THE MOST IMPORTANT THING A MAN CAN GIVE TO GOD APART FROM HIS HEART

THE MOST IMPORTANT THING A MAN CAN GIVE TO GOD APART FROM HIS HEART.

THE MOST IMPORTANT THING A MAN CAN GIVE TO GOD APART FROM HIS HEART

THE MOST IMPORTANT THING A MAN CAN GIVE TO GOD APART FROM HIS HEART.

THE MOST IMPORTANT THING A MAN CAN GIVE TO GOD APART FROM HIS HEART

THE MOST IMPORTANT THING A MAN CAN GIVE TO GOD APART FROM HIS HEART.

THE MOST IMPORTANT THING A MAN CAN GIVE TO GOD APART FROM HIS HEART

THE MOST IMPORTANT THING A MAN CAN GIVE TO GOD APART FROM HIS HEART.

THE MOST IMPORTANT THING A MAN CAN GIVE TO GOD APART FROM HIS HEART

THE MOST IMPORTANT THING A MAN CAN GIVE TO GOD APART FROM HIS HEART.

THE MOST IMPORTANT THING A MAN CAN GIVE TO GOD APART FROM HIS HEART

THE MOST IMPORTANT THING A MAN CAN GIVE TO GOD APART FROM HIS HEART.

THE MOST IMPORTANT THING A MAN CAN GIVE TO GOD APART FROM HIS HEART

THE MOST IMPORTANT THING A MAN CAN GIVE TO GOD APART FROM HIS HEART.

THE MOST IMPORTANT THING A MAN CAN GIVE TO GOD APART FROM HIS HEART

THE MOST IMPORTANT THING A MAN CAN GIVE TO GOD APART FROM HIS HEART.

THE MOST IMPORTANT THING A MAN CAN GIVE TO GOD APART FROM HIS HEART

THE MOST IMPORTANT THING A MAN CAN GIVE TO GOD APART FROM HIS HEART.

THE MOST IMPORTANT THING A MAN CAN GIVE TO GOD APART FROM HIS HEART

THE MOST IMPORTANT THING A MAN CAN GIVE TO GOD APART FROM HIS HEART.

THE MOST IMPORTANT THING A MAN CAN GIVE TO GOD APART FROM HIS HEART.

THE MOST IMPORTANT THING A MAN CAN GIVE TO GOD APART FROM HIS HEART

THE MOST IMPORTANT THING A MAN CAN GIVE TO GOD APART FROM HIS HEART.

THE MOST IMPORTANT THING A MAN CAN GIVE TO GOD APART FROM HIS HEART

THE MOST IMPORTANT THING A MAN CAN GIVE TO GOD APART FROM HIS HEART.

THE MOST IMPORTANT THING A MAN CAN GIVE TO GOD APART FROM HIS HEART.

THE MOST IMPORTANT THING A MAN CAN GIVE TO GOD APART FROM HIS HEART

THE MOST IMPORTANT THING A MAN CAN GIVE TO GOD APART FROM HIS HEART.

THE MOST IMPORTANT THING A MAN CAN GIVE TO GOD APART FROM HIS HEART

THE MOST IMPORTANT THING A MAN CAN GIVE TO GOD APART FROM HIS HEART.

THE MOST IMPORTANT THING A MAN CAN GIVE TO GOD APART FROM HIS HEART

THE MOST IMPORTANT THING A MAN CAN GIVE TO GOD APART FROM HIS HEART.

THE MOST IMPORTANT THING A MAN CAN GIVE TO GOD APART FROM HIS HEART

THE MOST IMPORTANT THING A MAN CAN GIVE TO GOD APART FROM HIS HEART.

THE MOST IMPORTANT THING A MAN CAN GIVE TO GOD APART FROM HIS HEART

THE MOST IMPORTANT THING A MAN CAN GIVE TO GOD APART FROM HIS HEART.

THE MOST IMPORTANT THING A MAN CAN GIVE TO GOD APART FROM HIS HEART

THE MOST IMPORTANT THING A MAN CAN GIVE TO GOD APART FROM HIS HEART.

THE MOST IMPORTANT THING A MAN CAN GIVE TO GOD APART FROM HIS HEART

THE MOST IMPORTANT THING A MAN CAN GIVE TO GOD APART FROM HIS HEART.

www.ingramcontent.com/pod-product-compliance
Lightning Source LLC
Chambersburg PA
CBHW051001060726
47593CB00018B/2023